## Dedication

I dedicate this journal to my baby brother, Ryan Montez Bell. Not a day goes by I do not miss your voice and your grand smirk. I truly know that your sudden and unexpected death, five years ago, walked me right into my purpose. It was time to get free. Time to get to know who I really am when no one is looking. I wish I had this journal when you left my world, and just maybe, I could have started breathing deeper a little sooner. Thank you for helping me let women know they are not alone, and a heart can mend without being ashamed.

Love Big Sis.
#RyanPrimetimebell

Thank you to those who have chosen my book to help jump start your journey to mental and emotional freedom. There is absolutely nothing wrong with you! Life happens, and I am proud you are ready to enhance you! Now...

#Comegetfreewithme

*Keondra Steagall*

## Acknowledgments

I would like to thank Myra Wilkinson at Wilkinson Family Therapy and MWilkinson Consulting, Chris Bond at Brandcocky, The Allison Family, and The Steagall Family.

## Preface

When I physically should have been dead, I lived. When my own mental anguish could have killed me, I lived. I lived to tell my story and hope to help *you* through *yours*. *You* see, I have realized that the things that I have been through prepared me to help you. I truly believe life's "bad stuff" makes us who we are. I hope in the next 30 days, you receive mental and emotional calmness. The Breaths you are taking start to really mean freedom to you. I hope this book jump starts your new you. The daily focus pages will help you stay focused and on the task on your hardest days. I want you to go back to this book and your writings and remember you are not alone. Also, to be able to look back to see how far you have come. Know that the first step to becoming a better you start with looking in the mirror and taking time to love yourself. Time with you helps to learn what you really like and are just okay with liking. Sometimes, going with the flow gets us stuck in something we truly do not want to be in. Time to remind yourself who you are in real life. These are original quotes from myself and bible verses I stood firm on. I remember when my ex-husband lost his job out of nowhere, our apartment caught on fire, my youngest brother died, my granny died, and my divorce was complete in a year. Talk about PTSD. These quotes and bible verses helped and still help me push through hard days now. The Focus list I created helped me deal with the anxiety attacks I was having, from work to the after-school program to pick up my children, less than 2 miles away. I remember writing "PICK UP YOUR KIDS" on my hand. Guess what?! I made it. When the superwoman had a hole in the cape, it took more than sewing the hole back together. It took getting in the mirror and truly pep-talking myself. I hope this book gives you your voice back, along with hope, peace, joy, and love of self.

#Snatchthat

## Day 1

I can remember the day I decided to be done with being mad. Mad at me, mad at my ex-husband, mad at my birth mom, shoot mad at my brother for dying, and mad at myself for putting up with things I just did not deserve. Forgiving myself for holding on to old stuff that truly meant nothing. I was tired of not sleeping and acting like I hated the world. To stop being mad was hard, forgiving me was even harder. But I forgave myself for wasting so much time and effort that could have been placed into really understanding and loving me.

Today, I forgive myself. There is no book for being a woman. There is only one moment at a time out of sadness and depression. No time limit on when and how to start loving you. But as for today, forgive yourself for mistakes you have made knowing and unknowingly. Forgive you for the mental and subliminal thoughts you have held onto. It is time for loving yourself, even if it is the hardest thing you do today. Today is a new beginning for a new you. A new way to become free.

**#Forgiveyou**

What are you forgiving yourself for today?

*I hope today is one of your best days - Keondra*

# Daily Focus

6am:_____

_____

7am:_____

_____

8am:_____

_____

9am:_____

_____

10am:_____

_____

11am:_____

_____

12pm:_____

_____

1pm:_____

_____

2pm:_____

_____

3pm:_____

_____

4pm:_____

_____

5pm:_____

_____

6pm:_____

_____

## Day 2

I Remember I was chasing after God's help because my life was just not right. Bishop T.D. Jakes had a "Woman Thou art loose" conference going on in Atlanta Georgia. The Bible verse leading the conference was Habakkuk 2: 2-3. I did everything it took to get there. I took a 3hr trip on a tank of gas and 60.00. After that conference, I focused on writing a plan and sticking to it.

I am focused: Focused on what makes me move. Focused on what my purpose is for today. That is, it is my purpose. No sidetrack, no call off. Focused on the mind, body, and soul.
Habakkuk 2 2-3 KJV
2- And the Lord answered me, and said, write the vision, and make it plain upon tables, that he may run that readeth it
3 -For the vision is yet for an appointed time, but at the end, it shall speak, and not lie: though it tarry, wait for it; because it will surely come, it will not tarry.

#Writetheplan

What is your plan?

*Today's plan is the start of something new - Keondra*

## Daily Focus

6am:_____

7am:_____

8am:_____

9am:_____

10am:_____

11am:_____

12pm:_____

1pm:_____

2pm:_____

3pm:_____

4pm:_____

5pm:_____

6pm:_____

_____

Day 3

There was a moment where I found myself running laps around my business parking lot. Things would be so heavy, and I could not sit still. I could not think straight, but I had to make sure things were in order for my kids. I had a sibling pulling on me hard. And the clients that I begged God to make happy. I can remember saying, "breathe girl, just breathe." It became a habit to say, "With every breath, I am healing." The funny thing is, I just reminded myself of this, this morning.

Today, I am not focusing on being broken. I am taking deep breaths, and with every breath I take, I am healing.

#BreatheNow

The reason you are breathing today is….

_____
_____
_____
_____
_____
_____
_____
_____
_____
_____
_____
_____
_____
_____
_____
_____
_____
_____
_____
_____
_____
_____
_____
_____

*Hoping today you breathe a little deeper -Keondra*

## Daily Focus

6am:_____

7am:_____

8am:_____

9am:_____

10am:_____

11am:_____

12pm:_____

1pm:_____

2pm:_____

3pm:_____

4pm:_____

5pm:_____

6pm:_____

_____

## Day 4

The days that everyone needed me, and I was no good for myself were the hardest. I was trying to pull myself out of the dark hole I was in. There are still days like this, but I take advantage of the sun and the wind. I take advantage of the moments I am in to feel the atmosphere. I enjoy one moment at a time. Life becomes busy, and we take for granted that tomorrow will be there.

Today, remember one moment at a time. One minute at a time. One hour at a time. Today is about me, feeling the air around me, and the sunlight that shines on my skin.

#Sunshineforone

I am thankful for the sun that shines around me because

_____
_____
_____
_____
_____
_____
_____
_____
_____
_____
_____
_____
_____
_____
_____
_____
_____
_____
_____
_____
_____
_____
_____
_____

*Enjoy this moment right here, right now, Breathe -Keondra*

# Daily Focus

6am:_____

7am:_____

8am:_____

9am:_____

10am:_____

11am:_____

12pm:_____

1pm:_____

2pm:_____

3pm:_____

4pm:_____

5pm:_____

6pm:_____

Day 5

As a little girl, I was told I would be nothing but a kitchen beautician, and that I would never provide for a family, and that is putting it nicely. I went to college because I feared the first part of my purpose. Just know that college did not work out because I was too busy doing hair. I Am PURPOSE. Hair is me. Point blank period!

Today, my head is held high because I am full of purpose. I will put my best foot forward in all I do today.

#Iampurpose

What is your purpose?

*I am standing in agreement with you and your purpose. -Keondra*

## Daily Focus

6am:_____

7am:_____

8am:_____

9am:_____

10am:_____

11am:_____

12pm:_____

1pm:_____

2pm:_____

3pm:_____

4pm:_____

5pm:_____

6pm:_____

## Day 6

I was so insecure and depressed, hearing "I love you" from others was hard and unbelievable. I was a woman who could not take a nice compliment from anyone. At some point, I realize I needed to tell myself that I love me. As a child, I did not hear the words, "I love you" often. I did not know until adulthood that I was supposed to hear those words daily. When I went through my divorce and was forced to be a mommy, I had to quickly understand the power of those three words and what they truly meant. I could not let that bitter seed take root and run deep.

Today, I will take my time to look in the mirror and tell me, "I love you."

#loveonyou

My best characteristics traits are

*Today do something just for you. -Keondra*

## Daily Focus

6am:_____

7am:_____

8am:_____

9am:_____

10am:_____

11am:_____

12pm:_____

1pm:_____

2pm:_____

3pm:_____

4pm:_____

5pm:_____

6pm:_____

_____

Day 7

A little while ago, I had to take custody of three nephews. Unexpectedly, I was also told that I was too weak and too broke to take on three children along with my two. Something inside of me would not let me allow another member of my family to experience what I did. At that moment, I went into #askagain mode. I went to the mirror, and I wrote in boldly, "today I am enough" because that day, I was the only one willing and qualified to take care of all five children.

Today, I am enough! Yes Me, I am more than enough.

#Morethanenough

I am more than enough because

___
___
___
___
___
___
___
___
___
___
___
___
___
___
___
___
___
___
___
___
___
___
___
___
___
___
___

*Today I am praying for a more than enough moment one that you stand tall in! – Keondra*

## Daily Focus

6am:_____

7am:_____

8am:_____

9am:_____

10am:_____

11am:_____

12pm:_____

1pm:_____

2pm:_____

3pm:_____

4pm:_____

5pm:_____

6pm:_____

_____

Day 8

There came a point in dating where I felt that I was irritating God, I kept asking him for the same thing. I was embarrassed that nothing ever worked out. I felt God would place good guys in my life, but the relationships did not work out. I tried to go out of my way to make the relationship work without much success.

I asked myself: Did I ask for too much? Did I mishandle God's plan? Because I gave so freely, did I expect too much in return? Was my love language too much? I had truly worked on myself and figured out what I needed and wanted in a relationship. So, I gave up, and I stopped asking for companionship.

A few months after the breakup, I then had a client prophesy to me as she was in my salon chair, everything; I had written on my mirror, reminding me that it was okay to want a healthy relationship. God had spoken to her about me. She then told me to ask God again for the desires of my heart. Writing at this moment makes tears stream.

Today, I will not be Embarrassed to ask God again for what I desire.

#Askagain

I need to ask again for

*The God we serve knows our heart's desires. Today, just ask him-*

*Keondra*

# Daily Focus

6am:_____

7am:_____

8am:_____

9am:_____

10am:_____

11am:_____

12pm:_____

1pm:_____

2pm:_____

3pm:_____

4pm:_____

5pm:_____

6pm:_____

_____

Day 9

I still have bad days that remind me that my childhood was hell. There is no way adult life will be that way. Every day, God shows himself and his plan. I say left, and He says right. Go figure. I tell you; I go his way even when it is the unknown. I have forced things that I wanted my way and failed. I now go with God's plan because the life I live today, I could not have dreamed of!

God has something better for me:
Jeremiah 29:11 (NIV) "For I know the plans I have for you," declares the Lord, "plans to prosper you and not to harm you, plans to give you hope and a future."

#Godsplan

Better for me looks like

*I hope your future has love, abundance, joy, and peace. -Keondra*

# Daily Focus

6am:_____

7am:_____

8am:_____

9am:_____

10am:_____

11am:_____

12pm:_____

1pm:_____

2pm:_____

3pm:_____

4pm:_____

5pm:_____

6pm:_____

_____

Day 10

For a long time, my self-esteem was nonexistent. I could not walk in a room full of women without wondering if they were prettier than me or better than me in some way. Why did they shine so brightly, and I could not shine at all?

Woooo! That was a very hard time for me. It took years for me to truly walk in my radiance- through self-talk, self-help books, and therapy, I am learning my value and my worth.

My smile and my walk are radiant. When I walk into a room today, I will light the way! I am the sunshine.

**#Iamradiant**

I light the way because I am....

*When you walk in the room today, I hope all see your beautiful face and your heart of gold. -Keondra*

# Daily Focus

6am:_____

_____

7am:_____

_____

8am:_____

_____

9am:_____

_____

10am:_____

_____

11am:_____

_____

12pm:_____

_____

1pm:_____

_____

2pm:_____

_____

3pm:_____

_____

4pm:_____

_____

5pm:_____

_____

6pm:_____

_____

## Day 11

  I remember being a school age kid and having to introduce myself. Everyone else had creative ways to introduced themselves and there I sat feeling unheard, unimportant, and invisible. I did not understand how to use MY voice, but when I did, I was empowered! I still practice introducing myself in the mirror, so I never forget who I am.Life can be a whirlwind and can take you from one place to another, from extreme emotions including sadness, worrying, anxiety, pain, and happiness. In those moments there is no one there but you and God. I have learned to use my own shovel to empower myself. I am strong, I am healed, I deserve happiness, my space consists of joy, I am light. I am kind, I deserve love, I am a necessity, my hands heal others, my words love, I am beautiful, my skin is perfect, and I am the blessing.


Sometimes you must put power back in your words. You must take control of the moment in your life. When your mind starts to wonder, and you start to doubt yourself! Bring you back to life takes determination, strength, and fight.

#Iam

I am

*Every time you walk in a room, remember who you are. -Keondra*

# Daily Focus

6am:_____

7am:_____

8am:_____

9am:_____

10am:_____

11am:_____

12pm:_____

1pm:_____

2pm:_____

3pm:_____

4pm:_____

5pm:_____

6pm:_____

_____

Day 12

It has been hard for me to identify as being successful. I have been told throughout life that I was not able to be successful as a stylist and will not be financially stable. I realized that I was hiding who I was because like-minded people did not surround me. I was around people who wanted me to live paycheck to paycheck when I could be a financially successful business owner.

I remember my pastor preached years ago about financial planning. He introduced the congregation to a panel of financially successful people who were able to move from the bottom to the top by writing out a plan. I applied this strategy to my life. I wrote out my financial plan, and I placed my plan in the Bible on Habakkuk 2: 2-3 and reviewed it monthly. Throughout this process, I was hungry, angry, stressed out, and begging, but I noticed that opportunities started to come my way. When I made up my mind to be successful, I had deliberated and could not procrastinate. I was able to accept what God had for me.

Today, I will not hide who I am. I will sit back and appreciate what I have accomplished, and I will enjoy every moment.

#Iamsuccess

What does success look like for you?

*Success comes to those who do the work-Keondra*

# Daily Focus

6am:_____

7am:_____

8am:_____

9am:_____

10am:_____

11am:_____

12pm:_____

1pm:_____

2pm:_____

3pm:_____

4pm:_____

5pm:_____

6pm:_____

_____

Day 13

There was a time when my family had experienced so much heartbreak and sadness. The energy I felt was so raw and so heavy, I did not want to get out of my bed. I remember being on an online prayer call one morning, and boy, I was down, during prayer, I walked around my entire house and physically snatching all my happiness back out of the air. Can you imagine, just running up the stairs, down the stairs, to the laundry room and the kitchen. I am sure my kids were hiding in the mist. But sometimes, it takes all that!

Today, I will snatch back all that was lost. All the wonderful seeds I have planted will be watered. I will receive my joy, my peace, my happiness, and my balance back today.

**#Snatchthat**

I am the author of how smooth my day will be. I will only accept the best of

_____
_____
_____
_____
_____
_____
_____
_____
_____
_____
_____
_____
_____
_____
_____
_____
_____
_____
_____
_____
_____
_____
_____
_____

*This is your day! -Keondra*

# Daily Focus

6am:_____

_____

7am:_____

_____

8am:_____

_____

9am:_____

_____

10am:_____

_____

11am:_____

_____

12pm:_____

_____

1pm:_____

_____

2pm:_____

_____

3pm:_____

_____

4pm:_____

_____

5pm:_____

_____

6pm:_____

_____

Day 14

When my divorce was finalized, I kept thinking I am supposed to feel free. I physically knew the burden was lifted. The physical pain that I was in was gone, but the mental prison remained. I had been codependent for so long, I did not know how to be free. I did not know how to just care about me. I had to walk myself through freedom one day at a time. I finally realized free looks like ME.

Today, I am free. If no one else chooses to be free today, I am still free.

#Freelookslikeme

What does freedom look like to you?

*You, Queen, are who decides what your freedom looks like. -Keondra*

# Daily Focus

6am:_____

7am:_____

8am:_____

9am:_____

10am:_____

11am:_____

12pm:_____

1pm:_____

2pm:_____

3pm:_____

4pm:_____

5pm:_____

6pm:_____
_____

Day 15

I remember the night I drove home with my newborn son and my three-year-old daughter. When I made it home, my water was turned off. I put my kids back in the car and drove to the dollar general store. I purchased two jugs of water to boil for the kids bath, and I stole a pack of diapers for my son. I cried all the way back home and begged God to forgive me.

That night was the first time I wrote on my mirror. "This isn't the plan God has for my family." This was also the first time I learned to biblically fast and seek God's face. I needed him to step in, or I was going to jump off the ledge.

I will not look at my circumstances today. I will remember God's promise. Romans 8:28 (NIV) and we know that in all things, God works for the good of those who love him, who[a] have been called according to his purpose.

#Morethanapromise

Standing firm on the vision of the life you have looks like…

*I truly believe all things come together for those who love the Lord. - Keondra*

## Daily Focus

6am:_____

7am:_____

8am:_____

9am:_____

10am:_____

11am:_____

12pm:_____

1pm:_____

2pm:_____

3pm:_____

4pm:_____

5pm:_____

6pm:_____

## Day 16

  As I learned who I was as a woman, I began to set good boundaries. Before setting boundaries, I was giving so much of myself to others but was not receiving anything in return. The more I set boundaries, the lonelier I felt. I knew that I had to love me more and stand up for how I deserved to be treated. I had to learn to love me.

  As I loved me more, I began to realize what I was giving out was light, love, and healing. I decided to remind myself every day that I will only put my energy and my love into what gives me the same energy and love back period.

I love me, and today I am going to make sure I feel the same love I give to others. My love- it is incredible. My love is honest, my love is genuine, and I deserve everything back that I give out.

#Ilovesomeme

What time are you taking for you as you set new boundaries today?

*I hope the time you take there is a much-needed bubble bath it will give you a moment of peace and quiet as you enjoy you.- Keondra*

## Daily Focus

6am:_____

7am:_____

8am:_____

9am:_____

10am:_____

11am:_____

12pm:_____

1pm:_____

2pm:_____

3pm:_____

4pm:_____

5pm:_____

6pm:_____

## Day 17

I remember when I made the decision to divorce my husband. I wanted the divorced but emotionally, I was depressed because of the uncertainty that this choice will bring. I had to stand firm on my choices and make an executive decision regardless of what others said. I was being told to stay with him because of our family dynamics and how we looked together. People used my past against me to try to convince me to stay in an unhealthy marriage. I needed to choose to be happy with myself and let go of the need to please my husband and others.

In the end, I decided to divorce him. I had to tell myself everyday that I was happy with my decision. I had to trust myself to make it through the loneliness and heal- mentally, physically, emotionally, and spiritually.

Today, I am happy because I choose to be happy! No matter what my circumstances are, no matter what the world says, I am supposed to be at this time. I am going to operate in this happiness!

#HappyWithMe

What about today makes you happy with yourself?

*Today's happiness is important. -Keondra*

# Daily Focus

6am:_____

_____

7am:_____

_____

8am:_____

_____

9am:_____

_____

10am:_____

_____

11am:_____

_____

12pm:_____

_____

1pm:_____

_____

2pm:_____

_____

3pm:_____

_____

4pm:_____

_____

5pm:_____

_____

6pm:_____

_____

Day 18

    I was adopted by a white male when I was 15 years old. However, I stayed in contact with my biological family and was raised by a surrogate family, as well. When I was in the state's custody, I was in 9 different foster homes and was placed with some families more than once. I always felt like I did not fit in.
    I had to fit into many different cultures- racially, academically, and biologically. I also had to learn to trust others because they did not trust me. I was judged based on the choices that the adults in my life made and the circumstances that I was placed in.

Today, I accept my past; I am not embarrassed by my past. Without it, I would not be who I am today. I love who I am today!

**#IAcceptme**

Are you ready to accept who you are?

*I am hoping today you are reminded why you should accept who you are! –*

*Keondra*

# Daily Focus

6am:_____

7am:_____

8am:_____

9am:_____

10am:_____

11am:_____

12pm:_____

1pm:_____

2pm:_____

3pm:_____

4pm:_____

5pm:_____

6pm:_____

_____

# Day 19

Before I decided to divorce my husband, we had one vehicle. My ex-husband was unemployed for three months, and during that time, we developed a routine. He would drop me off at work, the kids off at daycare and spend the day at home, "looking for a job." My ex-husband refused to pick me up from work after 8 pm. I had to pay for a taxi weekly to get home safely.

The taxi driver saw the car parked in the back of the house and began to ask me questions that I did not ask myself. A stranger pointed out my worth and value. I began to ask myself, "Can I justify working 8-10 hours per day and not drive my car?" I began to understand how to set boundaries in my life. After being married for five years, this was the first time in my marriage that I was able to stand up for myself.

There is absolutely nothing wrong with me! I expect what I give out, and if others cannot give that to me in return- I will set boundaries. "There is nothing wrong with my boundaries or standards! "

**#Myboundariesmatter**

What does your standards and boundaries say about you?

*Stand firm on who you are and what you stand for. If you do not, no one else will. -Keondra*

# Daily Focus

6am:_____

7am:_____

8am:_____

9am:_____

10am:_____

11am:_____

12pm:_____

1pm:_____

2pm:_____

3pm:_____

4pm:_____

5pm:_____

6pm:_____

Day 20

I remember the first time as an adult, married with children. I went to the ocean. I feel that God speaks clearly to me when I am in the water. I was feeling so sad and down, I remember clearly that day, "I love you this much," as the waves kept coming to shore. "Keondra, loves yourself this much. Tomorrow may never come, and you must enjoy yourself, now!" Wow, I still get chills thinking about it. At that moment, I was learning to choose myself. I was scared, but I was confident in God.

I love myself enough to let go of the past. Tomorrow may never come, so today will be lived to its fullest.

#Ilovememore

What reminds you to love yourself each day?

*Let today remind you of your purpose! -Keondra*

# Daily Focus

6am:_____

7am:_____

8am:_____

9am:_____

10am:_____

11am:_____

12pm:_____

1pm:_____

2pm:_____

3pm:_____

4pm:_____

5pm:_____

6pm:_____

_____

## Day 21

"Spaghetti Back!" No identity, no voice, no spine, just all over the place being manipulated. I spent a lot of my life physically sick, trying to please and make others happy. I was having chronic stomach problems, horrible headaches, and I felt disconnected. Because of my declining health, I had to decide between life and death. I had to define what was important in my life. I had to choose my happiness.

I will always define my happiness. Family, friends, nor any type of social media platform can decide what makes me, ME. This is My happiness.

#mylifemyhappiness

What brings you happiness in life?

*Never let the world describe your happiness!* -Keondra

## Daily Focus

6am:_____

7am:_____

8am:_____

9am:_____

10am:_____

11am:_____

12pm:_____

1pm:_____

2pm:_____

3pm:_____

4pm:_____

5pm:_____

6pm:_____

# Day 22

At some point, enough is enough. To feel good about myself, I wanted to be needed, but I did not have my STUFF together. I did not have a routine with my kids, my business was not growing, and financially, I did not have a plan. After my divorce, I was insecure about being abandoned, but I pretended that I was okay. By being there for others, I was able to distract myself from my truth

After six months of pretending to be okay, I began to feel overwhelmed because even though I was busy during the day taking care of others, I still had to deal with my personal STUFF at night. I remember crying at night because I felt stuck, rejected, and lonely. I did not know who I was or who I was becoming. I was tired of waking up every morning and feeling empty. I needed to take my own advice and be there for myself like I was trying to be there for others.

Today, I will not be codependent; everyone else's stuff will not consume me. I control my atmosphere, and it is my job to need me first. It is my job to love me first, to be whole first, before I can help with someone else's STUFF. And I do not feel guilty about that.

#controlyourself

What can you let go of today to become a better you?

*Stay in your lane; I promise you will feel so much lighter. -Keondra*

# Daily Focus

6am:_____

7am:_____

8am:_____

9am:_____

10am:_____

11am:_____

12pm:_____

1pm:_____

2pm:_____

3pm:_____

4pm:_____

5pm:_____

6pm:_____

Day 23

I had to make every day the best day of my life, regardless of what was going on. I had to believe it every day.

Today is the best day of my life. Period!!!

**#Ichoosetoday**

What has been one of the best days of your life?

*The most high has not forgotten you. -Keondra*

# Daily Focus

6am:_____

_____

7am:_____

_____

8am:_____

_____

9am:_____

_____

10am:_____

_____

11am:_____

_____

12pm:_____

_____

1pm:_____

_____

2pm:_____

_____

3pm:_____

_____

4pm:_____

_____

5pm:_____

_____

6pm:_____

_____

# Day 24

    I remember trying to find encouragement after a breakup. I was told by a friend that I was not worthy of a healthy relationship, and that is saying it nicely. At that moment, I begin to reflect on the relationship that this person and I had. I noticed that my "friend" was only there for me when I was down and out. It seemed as if she only wanted to be my friend when I felt bad about myself to make herself feel better. I realized that I needed to protect myself even if it meant that I must cut others out of my life.

    When I began to cut others out of my life, the loneliness started to take over. I realized that I allowed others to suck the life out of me through manipulation, selfishness, and emotional abuse. For protection, I learned to set boundaries and speak up for myself. I gained mental and emotional freedom.

I am not a selfish person, but I will protect my heart and my mind from selfish people. I will protect my ears, eyes, heart, and soul. No one will protect and care for me as I do myself.

**#Protection**

What are you reminded of today that needs to be protected?

*There is nothing wrong with choosing you first. -Keondra*

# Daily Focus

6am:_____

7am:_____

8am:_____

9am:_____

10am:_____

11am:_____

12pm:_____

1pm:_____

2pm:_____

3pm:_____

4pm:_____

5pm:_____

6pm:_____

Day 25

There are many times as women we deal with self-esteem issues. Through comparison and judgment, we begin to measure our worthiness based on what others have or their appearance. At some point, I realized that I did not have to compare myself to others to be happy or to feel like I am good enough.

A lot of days, I had to remind myself how my crown is supposed to sit. Not tilted nor cocked to the side, it is to sit perfectly on my lofted head right in line with a smile so radiant I light the room as I walkthrough. There are some days I am still reminding Keondra who she is.

Today, the crown on my head is held high. The beautiful smile I walk in the room with, leaves a lasting impression. Once again, I am the prize, and I deserve to be treated as such.

#Radiancelookslikeme

Describe what Radiance looks like to you....

*Look in the mirror and remind yourself of whom, you are. -Keondra*

## Daily Focus

6am:_____

7am:_____

8am:_____

9am:_____

10am:_____

11am:_____

12pm:_____

1pm:_____

2pm:_____

3pm:_____

4pm:_____

5pm:_____

6pm:_____

_____

Day 26

Listen, when I tell you that there have been some rough days along this journey called life. I need you to hear me when I say this. "Sometimes, God will break you to remind you who is in control." I spent a lot of days asking for self-love help. God stepped in and showed his grace.
I love myself more and more every day.

Lord, thank you for loving me when I did not love myself.

**#Grace**

How has God shown his grace on your journey?

*I promise God's Grace is sufficient. -Keondra*

## Daily Focus

6am:_____

7am:_____

8am:_____

9am:_____

10am:_____

11am:_____

12pm:_____

1pm:_____

2pm:_____

3pm:_____

4pm:_____

5pm:_____

6pm:_____

_____

Day 27

Many days I ask why me? Why am I not close to my parents like others? Why didn't I get the grandparents others had? Why didn't my marriage last? Why don't I have a romantic partner? Others divorced and married 1yr later. Blah blah blah. A bunch of complaining I needed to stop doing. Complaining got me nowhere but angry and bitter, and becoming something I did not want to be. Because of the love I found for myself, I am here today in a much healthier place in my heart and mind. Talk about lemons to lemonade.

Life happens! Today, I will not be mad about the hand I Was dealt; I will make this hand work for me.

#Iplaymyhandbetter

What will you do to make life work best for you?

*Make the decision to make the hand God dealt you worth living for. - Keondra*

# Daily Focus

6am:_____

7am:_____

8am:_____

9am:_____

10am:_____

11am:_____

12pm:_____

1pm:_____

2pm:_____

3pm:_____

4pm:_____

5pm:_____

6pm:_____

## Day 28

    In my codependent stage- I was no good. I was spewing neediness. I found myself stepping in the way of what God wanted for others. And I was getting the crappy end of the stick. I learned the hard way many times I must get out of the way. As I fixed my heart and mind -spiritually, mentally, and emotionally, I no longer hop in lanes I do not belong in.

I will no longer lose myself in others. My wellbeing is just as important as theirs. If I am not good with me, how can I be good for them?

**#Getoutoftheway**

How do you plan to keep yourself in your own lane from now on?

*Focus on you; be happy with that. -Keondra*

# Daily Focus

6am:_____

_____

7am:_____

_____

8am:_____

_____

9am:_____

_____

10am:_____

_____

11am:_____

_____

12pm:_____

_____

1pm:_____

_____

2pm:_____

_____

3pm:_____

_____

4pm:_____

_____

5pm:_____

_____

6pm:_____

_____

Day 29

I had to witness so many negative moments in my life that made me question who I was as a person. I was treated unfairly, and many times, I was powerless as I watched others being treated unfairly as well. As I faced the truth about life, I learned that you reap what you sow.

Many days, I have written the "Golden Rule" on my bathroom mirror. I had to keep reminding myself to be nice amid a mess. Or in the midst of messiness, I should say. It is easy to come apart when you are truly going through, but as you heal, you realize there are more unhealthy people in this world than we know. When you do the right thing, goodness just follows.

I will not accept mediocrity. I will not accept a little bit here and a little bit there. I will not accept anyone not treating me like I treat them. The "Golden Rule" is powerful.

#Thegoldenrule

Who will you introduce the golden rule to today?

*Set your deal breakers today with family ships, friendships, and relationships. It will be much easier to reach the golden rule then. -Keondra*

# Daily Focus

6am:_____

_____

7am:_____

_____

8am:_____

_____

9am:_____

_____

10am:_____

_____

11am:_____

_____

12pm:_____

_____

1pm:_____

_____

2pm:_____

_____

3pm:_____

_____

4pm:_____

_____

5pm:_____

_____

6pm:_____

_____

Day 30

    During my pain, my mirror became my best friend. I would write on it weekly, reminding God of what I needed and what he promised me. I reminded him I was a King's kid and not to forget me. I asked him to accept my praise to him in honoring who he is. I keep Not silent. You should not either.

Isaiah 62: 6-7 put God in remembrance of his promise. Keep not silent. Give him no rest until it comes to pass. Remind God again and again of his promise. Present your case and bring proof. He is faithful to his word. What God promised, he will do.

#AskAgain

What has God promised you that is still coming to fruition?

*By getting out of bed today, you have chosen to put your best foot forward. -Keondra*

# Daily Focus

6am:_____

7am:_____

8am:_____

9am:_____

10am:_____

11am:_____

12pm:_____

1pm:_____

2pm:_____

3pm:_____

4pm:_____

5pm:_____

6pm:_____

I am who I am with NO regrets. Thank you for starting something new and taking the first step to getting free with me.

**#Keondrasteagall**

www.ingramcontent.com/pod-product-compliance
Lightning Source LLC
Chambersburg PA
CBHW042308150426
43198CB00001B/5